Free Verse Editions
Edited by Jon Thompson

FIELD NOTES OF A FLANEUR

Lewis Meyers

Winner of the New Measure Poetry Prize

Foreword by Ellen Doré Watson

Parlor Press
Anderson, South Carolina
www.parlorpress.com

Parlor Press LLC, Anderson, South Carolina, 29621

Library of Congress Cataloging-in-Publication Data

Names: Meyers, Lewis author | Watson, Ellen, 1950- writer of foreword
Title: Field notes of a flaneur / Lewis Meyers ; foreword by Ellen Doré
    Watson.
Description: Anderson, South Carolina : Parlor Press, 2026. | Series: Free verse
    editions | Summary: "Field Notes of a Flaneur is a collection of fifty-four
    free verse poems. These poems feature keen observation of the gratifications
    and the troubles of human life as well as its many ambiguities"-- Provided
    by publisher.
Identifiers: LCCN 2025049501 (print) | LCCN 2025049502 (ebook) | ISBN
    9781643175560 paperback | ISBN 9781643175577 adobe pdf | ISBN
    9781643175584 epub
Subjects: LCGFT: Free verse
Classification: LCC PS3613.E9846 F54 2026 (print) | LCC PS3613.E9846
    (ebook) | DDC 811/.6--dc23/eng/20251208
LC record available at https://lccn.loc.gov/2025049501
LC ebook record available at https://lccn.loc.gov/2025049502

2 3 4 5

Cover photo by Robert Bye on Unsplash.
Book design by David Blakesley.

Parlor Press, LLC is an independent publisher of scholarly and trade titles in
print and multimedia formats. This book is available in paperback and ebook
formats from Parlor Press on the World Wide Web at https://www.parlorpress.
com or through online and brick-and-mortar bookstores. For submission
information or to find out about Parlor Press publications, write to Parlor
Press, 3015 Brackenberry Drive, Anderson, South Carolina, 29621, or email
editor@parlorpress.com.

Contents

Contents

3

4

Foreword

As a poet, teacher, and poetry translator with a sideline in manuscript editing, I often meet people initially through their writing, and that's how I first met Lewis Meyers—but my acquaintance with him is unusual because I received his poems from his widow over a year after his death. Diana Tietjens Meyers had compiled a selection of her late husband's poems, and she sought me out to advise her about the merits of the poems she judged to be his best. Feeling wary, I agreed to take a look—and immediately recognized the lost voice of a true poet whose work deserved to be read widely. Thus began the partnership that resulted in the publication of *Field Notes of a Flaneur*.

Who Was Lewis Meyers?

Lewis Meyers was born in 1934 in Washington DC and lived there through his undergraduate years at George Washington University, where he first began writing poems. He attended poetry readings at the Institute of Contemporary Arts and the Library of Congress, where he recalled his excitement hearing Delmore Schwartz, Allen Tate, and John Crowe Ransom. While studying for an MA in American Studies at the University of Michigan, he joined poet-in-residence Donald Hall's circle of aspiring poets. In later years, he enjoyed telling stories about some of the visiting poets' shenanigans at the parties Hall hosted for them. But he was earnest about writing poems and civil rights activism on campus and in Detroit. His early writing met with success, with poems published in *Epos*, the *Hudson Review*, the *Paris Review*, and *Poetry Northwest*.

After completing his MA, Meyers moved to New York City, where his priorities shifted to resisting the illegal war the US was fighting in Vietnam. During the 1960s, he was a member of Angry Artists Against the War in Vietnam and participated in the Poets Caravan actions that the organization sponsored. Staying in touch with other poets and their work, he did a stint as poetry editor of the radical New York City weekly newspaper, the

Guardian. A founding member of Up Against the Wall Motherfuckers, he proposed the group's name (taken from a line in Amiri Baraka's 1967 poem "Black People"). Eventually, Meyers began performing with the Sixth Street Theater, as well as continuing to participate in mass demonstrations against the war. Early in 1970 after a cross-country tour with the Sixth Street Theater ended in disbandment, he met his future wife, Diana Tietjens, in San Francisco. By August, they had decided to marry and settle in New York City, where he joined the English Department at Hunter College, and taught there for the rest of his teaching career.

In line with his convictions about social justice, Meyers advocated for expanding the English language canon and diversifying the department's curriculum to better serve the college's highly diverse students. Along the way, he published several innovative writing composition textbooks that focused on engaging the most challenged students. When not overwhelmed by his heavy teaching responsibilities and textbook projects, he wrote poems. Although he hardly ever submitted, he had great success when he did, publishing in *Field*, the *Antioch Review*, and the *Literary Review*.

After retiring in 2008, Meyers dedicated himself exclusively to writing poems but remained unmotivated to send them out. For the first five years of his retirement, he spent semesters in Chicago with his Diana, who had taken up a research professorship at Loyola University. The city had a leaden effect on his work. Dyed-in-the-wool New Yorker that he was, Meyers complained that Chicago provided little incident or inspiration for his writing. (During one tedious semester, he amused himself by dashing off a memoir of his life before 1970). However, like artist Joan Mitchell, who declared painting "indispensable . . . like an addiction," Meyers once told Diana that for him poetry was an "addiction." So, Chicago slowed him down but couldn't stop him. And when Diana retired in 2013, they happily resumed full-time residence in New York City, where Meyers's writing flourished. He died seven years later.

So thoroughly was Meyers's life suffused with poetry that when he learned that he had a fatal disease, he told his wife how he felt about it by handing her a book of W. S. Merwin translations, open to an anonymous Egyptian poem dating from the twentieth-century BCE. It begins:

> Death is before me today
> Like health to the sick
> Like leaving the bedroom after sickness.*

---

* *Selected Translations: 1948–1968.* W. S. Merwin. Atheneum, New York (1969), p. 3.

By the time of the COVID pandemic when urban dwellers were mostly confined to their apartments, Meyers's eyesight had deteriorated so grievously that he found it barely possible to read from his voluminous home library of poetry, fiction, and history. Eighty-six years old and almost deprived of one of his greatest pleasures in life, he solemnly and clear-headedly acceded to his own death.

How This Book Came to Be

Meyers continued working on revisions of existing poems and drafting new ones until a few weeks before dying on December 28, 2020. Near the end of his life, he let Diana know of his wish that she endeavor to publish his best work posthumously. After many hard months of bereavement, she was finally able to begin reading and sorting the six-inch stack of poem printouts he had left on his desk. By early in 2022, she had organized a selection of these poems into a sixty-page manuscript. Certain that her late husband would want only his most worthy poems to be published, and aware of her own limitations as a philosopher with only undergraduate schooling in the literary arts, she sought out a poetry editor to help her keep her promise.

And so it was that Diana's query letter came to me, and I met Lewis Meyers through his poems—though, before I sat down to read, it struck me as a very, very long shot that I'd find a manuscript by a deceased poet with a few publications worth championing, much less appealing enough for a press to publish it.

But I was utterly swept away! After just a handful of poems, I settled in and read from start to finish. It felt like a delicious visit with a totally idiosyncratic, dark, and delightful mind. Though his style is more expansive, Meyers's work has much in common with Charles Simic's, containing healthy pinches of wickedness, wit, and metaphysical wisdom. I felt lucky to have been tapped for this project.

As requested, I offered Diana advice about poems that didn't stand up quite as well as others; she sent along a group of poems she'd not included in the manuscript, some of which we added in. Later, she discovered another enormous cache of poems on Meyers's computer. Among them she found promising pieces we'd not yet considered, a goodly number of which turned out to be clear keepers. The manuscript grew and changed.

We did not see ourselves as editors or improvers. In fact, we did precious little meddling with the poems themselves. Ours was a partnership—between a poet guide and the person who knew Lewis and his work better than anyone else—with the goal of gathering his strongest poems to come together as a book to represent his life's work. I am by trade a poet/editor/ teacher, but there was nothing to teach here. Lewis was a complete poet (and I learned a few things from him along the way).

Diana had assumed she would need to self-publish a book of Meyers's poems but, in my estimation, they deserved better—deserved readers! With help from Barbara Ras, my closest and most trusted poet friend, I hatched a plan to shepherd Meyers's poems into print at a reputable press. First, we would need to demonstrate the appeal of his work to today's readers and editors. So, with Diana's enthusiastic assent, I began submitting to journals. To date, eleven more of Meyers's poems have been published—in no less than *The Paris Review, Poetry Northwest, Five Points, Hudson Review, Massachusetts Review, Plume,* and *Arkansas International.* This positive reception from top-flight journals confirmed my sense that Meyers's voice speaks to current editors and readers—but without a living poet to embody the poems, book publication would be a greater challenge.

It struck us that we might improve the odds if we could find renowned, prominent poets excited enough about Meyers's work to agree to participate in a series of live or Zoom readings to celebrate the book's publication. And we did! Poets from across the diverse spectrum of contemporary poetics responded to the call: Alicia Ostriker, Anne Marie Macari, Jessica Jacobs, Barbara Ras, Carolyn Forché, Chase Twichell, Christopher Merrill, Cole Swensen, Dana Levin, Eleanor Wilner, Kevin Prufer, Aracelis Girmay, Martha Rhodes, Marianne Boruch, Matthew Zapruder, and Tim Seibles all read a selection of Meyers's poems and signed on enthusiastically to become supporters of the book, sending along encouraging comments: "I'm hooked!" "A real discovery!" "Strange and wonderful!" and "I love these poems—so sharp and pointy and smart and moving."

Lewis Meyers's Cultural and Thematic Affinities

Meyers's eclectic tastes in literature, the visual arts, and music, and the sensibilities they bespeak, reflect his personality, which in turn shaped his writing. In literature, he admired Kafka above all others. But he held many other writers in high esteem: F. Scott Fitzgerald, Isaac Babel, Elizabeth Bowen, Ford Madox Ford, and J. D. Salinger, not to mention classic Chinese and Japanese poetry and prose. He also read history, both political and military. He loved film noir as well as the films of Ingmar Bergman and the Coen Brothers. Outside these bodies of work, his favorite movies were *The Thief of Bagdad* (1940) and *Bringing Up Baby* (1938). He listened to Baroque chamber music, Bach, Mozart, and Haydn when he wasn't grooving to boogie-woogie or Blondie. In painting, he was enthralled by Piero Della Francesca as much as by Cezanne, Mondrian, Rothko, and Hodgkin. You may well detect traces of these capacious but discerning affinities as you read his poems.

The Freshness, Complexity, and Offbeat Brilliance of Lewis Meyers's Poems

As the title *Field Notes of a Flaneur* suggests, this collection features keen observation of the pleasures and dilemmas of human life, as well as its sorrows, injustices, and ambiguities. Fittingly, tone and mood range across delight, perplexity, and anguish. As wise as these poems are (and they are), the voice is young, surprises itself, refuses to sit down and behave. Innocence and discernment cohabit here.

One of my favorite poems in the book, "Summer Letters," reveals Meyers's knack for brief, startling images / realizations delivered in very few words. To give you a taste of what this book has to offer, I offer a little selection of amuse-bouches to tantalize your poetry palate:

> Choral mushrooms.
>
> Tree, the sun's brainchild.
>
> Wind bends the tree. I couldn't do that.
>
> Rain. The Saplings. It skins them alive.
>
> Deplorably rocky meadows.
>
> ("Summer Letters")

Deplorably—what a hoot! This poem seems to me to be born of meticulous attention married to a relaxed and open imagination. Line after line, I stop to laugh, linger, take pleasure, and wonder further at his surprising formulations.

"Satan Flaneur" was the lead-off poem in the first version of the manuscript that Diana sent me. Though we decided it was better placed a little further in, I'm glad it was the first thing I read, because it was like nothing I'd ever seen before: rangy and wry and fresh and idiosyncratic. When I came up for air after its four pages, I was wide awake and ready for more, thinking this poet is *wily*. In simple, direct language he introduces many conundrums. And it struck me that one of his strengths was the ability to shift scale without losing a beat. Ostensibly unrelated three-line vignettes—a bit like Haiku— jump from here to there, from first to third person, surveying the riot of incongruity, disappointment, misapprehension, nostalgia, and real or imagined peril that unsettles everyday life. Here are three delicious bits that may rise to appetizer-size:

> A flooded ditch pushes through the brush lands.
> Only because a snowy egret visits it
> is the water forced to turn blue.

> Does it matter whether Bohm or Bach
> wrote this piece for organ?
> Whether I lived or you did?

> I smile as my mind lights
> on the right thing to think of
> of all the things to think.

> When a wind rises
> wind chimes
> have no choice.

("Satan Flaneur")

In contrast to the artfulness of the synergistic poems above, consider this carefully constructed piece:

Glazier

> The glazier's men bear away
> a wood-framed sail-sized
> pane of the sky after a rainstorm.
> Some will look at it, others through.
> But tilt now and let in cars and sudden buildings,
> ruining the vision, along with lampposts and people.
> And how badly it would reflect on us
> should one of this two-man crew stumble
> into darkness. He won't. In the light of day,
> we see how it's possible to use muscle
> to achieve balance within reason
> though clouds hold religiously to their position
> above and the desired clarity of mind

is stricken by some obstreperous body.
So the heavens pass on our level
filling the glass in the hands of men
who hold on. They share its transparence
when the sun breaks into the picture
the pane makes without cracking it.

So much more is going on here than the recounting of the ordinary doings at a city worksite. To start with, the poem suggests that when it comes to looking, we all have a choice—to look *at* or *through*. Or, to change the angle utterly, allowing more into our sightline. But this is potentially dangerous: if, over and above ruining the vision before us, there could be collateral damage. Sit with that for a while, in a little poem in which window installers unwittingly create a heavenly tableau in the course of their job! But the poem pushes further: if one of the workers holding this immense piece of glass were to "stumble into darkness," that *would reflect badly on us*. I enjoy the pun on "reflect," and I sense that I'm meant to consider whether or not rubber-neckers (we readers?) are to be held blameless. And we're only half-way through the poem. Every bit of it asks us to think miles behind and beyond the words and their measured tone.

The speaker assures us that the man *won't* stumble, because it's day-light, and muscle can assure balance ("within reason"), though doubt creeps back, since the faithful clouds are not committed to sticking around. (Are they the "obstreperous body" in the way of clarity?) Next, the "heavens come down to our level." After sitting with that for a bit, I return to see that the heavens are "filling the glass in the hands of men," who continue to "hold on" but, by doing so, they share with us the marvel of "transparence when the sun breaks into the picture / the pane makes." Well! I love how "picture," perched at the end of the line, seems to finish the phrase, but then hurtles on to extend and clarify: not only does the sun break into the picture the poem makes, but into the poem itself—a "breaking" that reveals the world whole.

Another characteristic I find winning about this book is that underlying the formal and tonal variety is an identifiable human voice. And while we don't find a whole lot of autobiographical material here, there are a number of poems drawn from the poet's life—what I'd call "small bite" poems with big impact, which—without apron-wringing—personalize abominable social realities. "Winifred," which looks back on growing up in Washington DC under Jim Crow segregation, accomplishes both in ten short lines:

Winifred

> Winifred our maid said
> the movie house on Kennedy
> Street is for white
> people like you Larry.
> I never heard that.

> Winifred our maid said
> she'd take me to see
> whatever is on at the matinee
> if I finished my American cheese sandwich.
> I heard that.

Winifred speaks from a place that young Larry (Meyers's nickname) doesn't yet know exists. I marvel that as a grown man, a political activist no less, he's able to frame this moment so simply and poignantly. Meyers's deep concern about injustice and lack of compassion is reflected in a range of poems, including "What Is in the Water" (militarism), "The Climate of Fascism," "Metatron's Journal" (terrorism)," "Originals" (colonialism), and "The Lion House" and "To Be" (homelessness). But lest these titles give you the impression that the poet might go all sanctimonious on you, I reassure you that never happens.

I also appreciate that this poet recognizes that suffering is real and matters, even if it's not operatic in scale. "The Moon Is Bourgeois" gently scoffs at middleclass aspirations at the same time that it cloaks them in the moon's luminosity. And the pathos in this little poem is short-lived but heart-rending.

Bird

> The daughter, unlearned as a bird
> when it comes to windows,
> walked into a glass door
> and bumped her smooth forehead.
> Soundlessly her mouth fell open.
> But not until her father swept her up
> in his arms and the few who looked on
> pronounced each one his Oh! of alarm,
> did she start in to cry. For herself, of course,

but also for you and me and for everyone
stopped by the air hardening against us.

Meyers's empathy extends to the non-human, as well:

> Turtle has her ear to the ground
> and curls her lip. She knows
> what's coming before we
> appear, and that it's not justice but force
> that tramps the earth and tramples
> the small washed-up creatures
> in the grass, in the forest,
> in their houses getting dinner going.

("In the Kingdom of the Chelonians")

We humans are notorious for exploiting nonhuman creatures, but Meyers sweetly gives a turtle the upper hand in this poem.

In a different mood, Meyers delights in treating readers to a comical dimension of suffering. This poem springs from his puckish side:

In the Kitchen

> Let's say there's a God
> and he has a kitchen.
> He invites you into it.
> He opens every drawer
> and takes out one cooking utensil
> after another. Look, he says,
> demonstrating each of them,
> how this one works, and that one.
> They grind, flatten, slice, mix, pound.
> Then he comes to the grater.
> He says notice the unique refinement
> each side has to offer.
> He leaves it at that
> but looks at you expectantly,
> hoping you'll comment.
> Unfortunately, the best you can do
> is to remember how it felt
> to skin your knees as a child.

Like a train, certain, eventually to rattle down the track, the closing section of the book looks at the last (or impending) moment of the "air hardening against us." Sometimes humorous, sometimes somber, these poems reflect how mortality plays out in our lives. Well-worn though the topic may be, Meyers opens unexpected perspectives, each poem embedding this ultimate existential reality in a novel and ingenious scenario. One of my personal favorites:

The Milkweed Diet

In the sixth chapter
God sets the Monarch
butterfly the task
of cracking a person's
lifeline with its two wings
when it's time.
In his prayer book
the old man reads
the Blessing for Milkweed,
every sterling thread of which
is essential to the Monarch's diet,
and his faith is tested.
He'd starve the insect
to go on living
endless hours, endless days.
Didn't the widows say he looked sixty?
In his book,
birds snap butterflies out of the air.
But one flutter
makes a stir and changes everything—
slightly, yet a little is enough
for God to turn his face from him.
The butterflies have started eating,
they're eating, it's over.

I can't imagine anyone reading this book cover-to-cover and *not* feeling as though they had "met" the remarkable man with gimlet eyes (Diana's words) who wanted us to read it. His final poem, "One Last Thing" (oh! the humor and shiver of the title—a man who knows he's on the way out the door) is strikingly clear and calm and "alive / to the concentration of emotion / in language." Despite worry and "wind-devils," the poem is both an Ars Poetica and a gracious farewell.

We are immeasurably grateful to Free Verse Editions that Lewis is heard and remembered.

Ellen Doré Watson

Acknowledgments

Arkansas International: "Bird" (forthcoming)

Five Points: "Advent," "Happiness," and "Another Room" (Spring 2023)

The Hudson Review: "Cy Twombly's Leda" and "Úbeda" (October 2023)

The Massachusetts Review: "The History of Earthworms," "The Climate of Fascism," and "In Country" (Summer 2024)

The Paris Review: "Summer Letters" (Summer 2023)

Plume: "Poor Fish" (forthcoming)

Poetry Northwest: "The Milkweed Diet" (Winter/Spring 2024)

Verse Daily; "Happiness" https://www.versedaily.org/2024/happiness.shtml

Ellen Doré Watson and Diana Tietjens Meyers wish to thank Barbara Ras and Kevin Prufer for their generous brainstorming, advice, and support over the course of working towards the publication of *Field Notes of a Flaneur*.

Field Notes of a Flaneur

1

Blindness

The blind girl hears the stone wall
her dog has marched her up to.
She stands forgiven for thinking
stones are air. Both stand there,
facing the situation as quietly
as the stone blocks did when first joined.
She smiles at them, not to offend.
On the far side, the St. Marks dead,
bridling at pavement they wish was grass,
like us had rushes of feeling once.
But they're no help at all now.
Shouldn't someone who has a heart
use his head and take a hand to help?
Yet girl and dog stare in pure Egyptian profile,
nerveless, and not giving offense.
It's just as if they were meant to be here,
as if the afternoon had been listening for them,
the shade trees cutting it short with the breeze.
People out in force for a little air
began to wonder where faith should lie,
finding a blind girl and her dog
standing as if enchanted, as if they
gazed at themselves in a mirror
where only the two of them were.

Happiness

On the coffin-sized back porch
high above the ground
where anyone worth his salt
pursued his heart's desire,
I didn't know what to do
and asked my mother that.
I was seven. It was August,
the Capital's glandular month;
it came in with morning glories
between its teeth, or darting eyes.
We were in a natural sweat.
My health took the heat off,
but not Baudelaire's boredom
which I wasn't aware I had.
Mother couldn't allay it,
but I thought it must be happiness,
the word on everyone's lips
just before the end of the world.
And I stood on the screened porch,
looking in on the kitchen
while mother made lunch
and *Tosca* played on the radio,
bored to tears of happiness,
or happily sweating with boredom.

Sighs

Settling into a chair after steps
mounting on steps to get here,
a person sighs, might sigh, eyes as lidded
as a buttercup's translucent shadow.

That's the buttercup you pick to hold
up to a heartthrob's bare throat.
If there's a shadow, then it's love.
Love whose geography is a sigh

spreading the languor of yellow
shadows in bed with the shades drawn.
So I am trying to persuade you
to wallow in shadow and rest in sighs.

That's the yellow of the children's buttercup.
And because you lost sleep (where is it?
it has its own life), I wrap my hands
around your wrists to draw you up,

carefully, without pulling. But you're afraid.
Of what? Of the river of days, I suppose,
half algae, curving under the biased trees.
Backsliding trees, prone to slipping down

the slope and into the drink. But I say
cast your bread upon the waters
and it will float and come back to you
yellow, softened, not waterlogged, sighing.

Summer Letters

Tree, the sun's brainchild.

The caterpillars are crawling to heaven.

The porcupine ate the delectable car tire.

Wind bends the tree. I couldn't do that.

The black raspberry's passion for a drop of sunlight.

While I wrote, a butterfly, that critic, rode my wrist.

Brown velvet gown trimmed in yellow with blue polka-dots.

A bird squeezed itself through the air.

A bird swallowed space and then exhaled it.

Rain. The saplings. It skins them alive.

A shotgun echoes despairingly from the valley.

Choral mushrooms.

Queen Anne's lace sweetens wild carrot breath.

The earth's rigid plates drift below the daisy.

Backgammon on grass, losing every game to ants.

The sun and clouds playing honeymoon bridge.

Creams and lotion. Brushes to apply the lesson.

Like the black lily that comes up year after year despite the hostility of the gardener.

To sleep like an opera star, still singing.

Deplorably rocky meadows.

Toadflax, orange and yellow, opposed to black's pure repulsion.

The cows' rustling mouths, but God will scatter their teeth.

The light is too dark for colors to help.

The grape is squashed in bitter prejudice.

Turtlehead, Indian pipe, purple bergamot, heal-all, bull-thistle!

The whitewashed wood snaps in exasperation.

Pearly everlasting is my girl.

Still Life and Motion

Through this bus window tonight,
the words *apples* and *onions* appear
and remind me of the things themselves.
But not in Cezanne's *nature morte*.
There the real leaves the actual behind
yet is all the more real for that.

I saw that happen also on a bus
in a worse time. Night's biting rejoinders
had won me over to its position.
Then a glass door lit in a blank wall,
a frame for women who swam in lanes.
Their white arms flashed against the blue.

Soundlessly they moved past, as I
moved with them, and I was gone
before they reversed. But the blue pool
consoled my exhaustion and cooled
the fever risen from losing the real
in words that were so far from the actual.

The swimmers in maillots and black
bathing caps, though separated
from me by window beyond window
and by the disappearances of motion,
were there in the flesh and were
beautiful, which is the most real.

Úbeda

I want the motorcade to vanish
into more than the end of the street.
I want it to be broken into fragments by the sun.
I want it to have been made entirely of hearses.

The select passenger's head lies on a silk cushion;
his nose sticks up like a dripless candle.
But release me from wanting anything,
yet why be ashamed to say where your heart is?

Put me down among the January roses
where a man on a bicycle rounds the corner to enter
the Street of the Moon and the Sun in Úbeda.

He rides into the wakening plaza and there dismounts.
The statue of the blind Angel of Innocence looks at him.
Children are shouting as the sun walks toward the sundial.

Cy Twombly's Leda

Everything goes haywire in a hail
of black lines representing the various
vibrating positions in time of Leda's hips
as she pumps up and down on the Swan
like the motorcycle parked outside
the gynecologist's office; she leaves
in her exhaust the solitary egg
that looked to impact her; it will take
an atom bomb to change me, she tosses
back with a laugh as she joins the traffic.

Lares

Right through the black stone
shoots the ambulance's blue light,
but I don't know a thing about it
where, in it, I've lain down.

That's my small round black stone,
by the way, my household god, in fact.
Never can I be without it
and still manage, wherever I am,
to be at home. It stands
in a closed glass jar and picks up
everything going on around it:
kitchen noises, voices
coming in from the street,
the street itself at considerable depth.

And me, looking at the ceiling
of the ambulance box
flying along an important avenue
under glass, tonight, in this black stone.

Nostalgia

It kept my tea warm
and fuming, nostalgia,
even as I went down the field
to pick wild strawberries
with my nose to the ground,
and then climbed back up again
and raised the cup to my lips
like the place between her thighs
after kissing their insides
shaking for what came next
that they remembered from before.

In Country

The sun has come to power.
Could it ever overstay its welcome?
But it may need to dissolve an aspirin
or two on earth in a piercing stream.

Before the day is over, at dusk,
the heavy drinker has fallen flat
on his face in his own garden.
Tsk-tsking in the grass; recriminatory

notes under the hoods of trees.
Yet a brown dog named However
has escaped its chain and ranges free;
he wants to take a raccoon by the hand.

Night now. Bats rob the cradle;
drops smaller than a needle's point tap
against a house's windowpanes.
Safe inside, in bed, a man reads Proust

aloud to a woman until they sleep.
But at the bottom of the road, dislike
of each other pushes another couple apart
and finally fells the remaining elm.

Will the sun change them back? It will not.
The two following Swann's Way scent
the unfolding flower of the sun
and are happy they're no one else.

The Moon Is Bourgeois

The moon is full of itself
and goes from triumph to triumph,
rising in the estimation

of every celebrity hunter.
Its glory is fleeting.
For a whole hour,

it can't exceed the limit
of my window,
and the earth never.

Yet it shrugs that off
as a necessary conciliation
of what lies beyond it.

Ultimately it's bourgeois,
like a vatic poet
in residence.

Last evening it passed
over a green field
lit by more than itself.

The way things stacked up
there, the players
were in hell, the crowd in heaven.

That was all right
with the moon if it was
all right with them;

it wasn't so high and mighty.
All it really wanted,
if it came down to it,

was to stay in town,

maybe start a business,
marry, join the citizens

in their daily life,
even become, in time,
a leading light.

I Feel Real Good

I feel real good,
as if I'd slept on a different star
and didn't have to dream
about what I and the others do.
Mental health after all,
after I swung open the medicine
cabinet door with its mirror also
on the inside surface, and at the same time
ran water in the sink.
This wasn't remarkable.
Nor were the twin
porcelain sinks and falling water.
This was as it should be.
But I found myself
to be of two minds, as they say
when they mean something else,
one on my left, one in another place.
This was new.
I stood there trying to think.
But thank my lucky stars
the moment passed.
Today, as I've said,
I'm back to my old self.

Sparrow

The English sparrow makes his debut
at a café facing the Hotel Terminus.
He swoops down like the basso profundo
who embraces a whole table in Vienna.
Pity the sparrow has to go under the table.

The customers, over coffee, talk over his head.
How practiced they seem, shaking the tiny sacks
of sugar before tearing them open to loosen the grains.
But he can hardly envy their hands.
All he wants is the superflux.

Is that too much to ask? He's dirt poor,
but do you see him messing in your dish?
He knows his place and what his limits are.
He has no clothes, no doctors, nothing.
He has no future because he has no past.

Because he can't weep, he doesn't laugh.
He makes me tired. It's this life of mine,
this life of feeding and drifting, to quote
Charles Baudelaire on those crowding
out Poe's shadow on the sidewalk.

And now the sparrow wings off like the god,
like Hermes who also appeared in the guise
of an ordinary person but, the story runs,
shied away from any human contact
when immanence began to pall on him.

Glazier

The glazier's men bear away
a wood-framed sail-sized
pane of the sky after a rainstorm.
Some will look at it, others through.
But tilt now and let in cars and sudden buildings,
ruining the vision, along with lampposts and people.
And how badly it would reflect on us
should one of this two-man crew stumble
into darkness. He won't. In the light of day,
we see how it's possible to use muscle
to achieve balance within reason
though clouds hold religiously to their position
above and the desired clarity of mind
is stricken by some obstreperous body.
So the heavens pass on our level
filling the glass in the hands of men
who hold on. They share its transparence
when the sun breaks into the picture
the pane makes without cracking it.

2

2

Satan Flaneur

Going over her golf game,
she says she has power but no control.
Poetry is always about something else.

What was on my mind
that moved the grocery clerk
to ask if I was all right?

Su, drunk one night in the eleventh century,
is my ideal, and Villon, killer and thief,
redeemed by criminality from the university.

Does it matter whether Bohm or Bach
wrote this piece for organ?
Whether I lived or you did?

Everyone should know what the traffic will bear.
To bring Alcestis back, mute as a flower,
Heracles must waylay Death offstage.

Twice driving in my life I turned too hard
on ice and got so turned around I was pointed
toward my birth instead of toward my death.

There's no sun in the city anymore,
the old lady complains. Her friend, disagreeing,
says the sun just doesn't shine so bright now.

A flooded ditch pushes through the brush lands.
Only because a snowy egret visits it
is the water forced to turn blue.

Someone is getting his key ready
outside the front door to come in
though no one is missing from the household.

I smile as my mind lights
on the right thing to think of
of all the things to think.

The old man's walker has a claw foot.
Such ferocity! But each toe
ends in a rubber tip.

When a wind rises
wind chimes
have no choice.

Who remembers what overwrought people
say at funerals that aren't ours?
We'd remember what they said at ours.

The sofa cushion accepts my hard head.
Its only complaint is goose feathers.
Some days life can't squeeze out a tear for me.

Blue cubes convulse
in black windows in lieu
of green lamps.

Most of the streets and houses I remember
are those I came across in dreams, not in life,
if by life we mean anything but dreams.

Sorrowfully I gaze out at the river.
In places, the algae are so widespread
the clear water seems the disease.

When did I see them last, the hunks of bread
and the small brown medicine bottle of schnapps
in my grandmother's black beaded handbag?

Scanning the face of a used compact disc
for scratches before buying it,
I saw the bad treatment I myself had received.

The blind man, feeling his way along,
sighed to think he was like anybody
who couldn't see what just wasn't there.

All on their deathbed
call for their mother,
who died calling for hers.

What will come back to you on your deathbed
is the dictum against attaching a sticker
to suede or leather.

We should bow to the dead,
not for what they made of themselves,
but for what became of them.

The Pope's body floats across Rome.
An inch below the stretcher-poles,
the dignitaries chat with the personages.

"He died so that me and my kids could be free,"
said Ms. Bedosky. "Is it right? Is it wrong?
It's not for me to say."

At the funeral, the white balloons
bobbing in the hands of the mourners
conveyed such messages as "Christ Lives!" and "So long, Leo."

"Lemon and lime, it's the same damn thing!"
"No, they grow on two different trees."
"I'm not going to argue with you, Mohamed."

Raised as a barbarian,
I sprinkled sugar on my meat,
which greatly impressed my host.

The person who could give me the axe
said he used to be a communist, too,
but now he has 24 sports jackets.

The dating service screens
for felons and marrieds,
but not for deadheads.

Mishandling my toy revolver,
I destroyed it immediately,
like everything else too good for me.

It's unreal when
everything is what it is
and not what it was.

I look at you but try not to let you see it,
like that helicopter never quite coming into view,
an eyeball with its trailing nerve.

Bird

The daughter, unlearned as a bird
when it comes to windows,
walked into a glass door
and bumped her smooth forehead.
Soundlessly her mouth fell open.
But not until her father swept her up
in his arms and the few who looked on
pronounced each one his *Oh!* of alarm,
did she start in to cry. For herself, of course,
but also for you and me and for everyone
stopped by the air hardening against us.

Believing in Angels

The reason to believe in angels,
who are beyond belief,
is not because they don't know what it is
to be chilled to the bone (they don't know
and run naked when one can see through the trees),
but it's to apprehend what they would

if they existed, doing so
most easily probably
in winter, a still season,
when everything stops to pose
for its photograph.

As for us,
we waddle
around in the cold, our nudes
buried in thicknesses of feathers.
And we carry
a comb for light-heartedness,
also, perhaps, an orange
balled in flimsy paper
to eat on a dark afternoon.

Angels would find it touching,
that we think we're still here.
They would be distantly amused,
yet eventually their lips would draw in
like dried flowers; they'd clap
their hands to their ears as we
make noises showing we're happy.
Which is the final reason
to believe in angels.

Roughness

Backing up a little
to let the bus pull in,
I leaned one hand
against a tree trunk
for balance. It was stable.
It was an upper Fifth
Avenue tree, preserved
to comfort the eyes of the rich
in the windows across the street.
But that isn't the tack
I wanted to take.
The uneven bark
rubbed my palm.
And I felt the way
exiles do after returning
to their native country.
I felt I'd come back,
after long absence,
to the roughness of things.

To Be

Cinders flee the banks
of the Old Fall River Line;
leaves on the bushes are taken aback
like the man who rode the rails.

He feels rushed settling in
on his mattress, the thousand-leaves,
the bed he made and must sleep in;
it's ample and thin. And it's night.

Turned turtle, his mind
wanders, his body laments.
His house is a pure hypothesis,
its walls an empty parenthesis.

But on all sides the blue presses in
between the trees like a curtain,
like a condolence, blown
on no wind, into what dream.

In the dream, his brothers smother him
with affection under their wing,
proclaim him: "Look, the dreamer cometh."
But it's morning. He's up and about.

Out somewhere, but he'll be back,
treading down the ants' mansion,
pulling the sky closed behind him,
as troublesome to himself as ever.

Newlyweds

The Just Married car sits on Addison,
its side-windows soaped with defiant slogans,
the chassis looking a little crushed by all the to-do;
it's taken up the same place for a week.

Behind what door in what near building
are the newlyweds talking at the moment?
Do they ever fall out of bed and go naked
to the window to check if they've got a ticket?

But old hands at marriage, humming, warn
that speculation is idle; it's wishful.
Look at their car more closely. It's hard to see in,
it's so low-slung, but the couple may still be in their seats.

Don't ask me why, but the smother, the suspected
aroma of the car's dimmed-out interior
comment on wedlock somehow. Cherry-red transparent dice
box St. Christopher's ears on the dashboard.

Or the couple simply ran off in different directions
once they'd pulled in, having seen the future—
their offspring sticking out at odd angles,
little square footage, a money honey door chime.

Wait. Say love is all after all. Let's say that.
Yet people passing the car on their sad way to work
still find their lips forming that half-smile
that comes when the case is uncertain.

In the Kitchen

Let's say there's a God
and he has a kitchen.
He invites you into it.
He opens every drawer
and takes out one cooking utensil
after another. Look, he says,
demonstrating each of them,
how this one works, and that one.
They grind, flatten, slice, mix, pound.
Then he comes to the grater.
He says notice the unique refinement
each side has to offer.
He leaves it at that
but looks at you expectantly,
hoping you'll comment.
Unfortunately, the best you can do
is to remember how it felt
to skin your knees as a child.

Another Room

The thing about space in paintings
is you can't step into it
to cough or kiss and cut
down an alley between the monuments.
Particularly that whiplash limit
sends you reeling
in Pieter de Hooch's paintings
where the door is always open

to another room, another chance in life,
but you can't go through that door.
You may make out a dresser's
edge in the pointless light.
There can be, hidden from view,
bed and bedstead and mirror.
And a woman showing her teeth
as she bites a thread in two,

mending all. That's as may be;
the dream consoles you. But at your peril,
and in place of your soul's desire
for the air to reveal
to you where it bends so you
can turn an invisible corner
into something else and see what gives there,
see past seeing.

Planets

My shooters and puries
came to hand and
slipped through my fingers.
The marbles rolled on
like uncontrolled worlds
the hand of God threw out
before he got the knack.
But it was only me.
These heavenly bodies
swirled with gaseous colors:
blue, cream, yellow, green.
They may still be in motion;
or on one bad luck day
they all were ground to dust.
But, in my universe of that era,
they clicked, and I watched
as one I'd aim and shoot
sent the cataclysmic other
hurtling forward,
taking me with them toward
a space that kept growing
away from me but that in time
I was supposed to fill.

The Comeback

Then the sparrow I killed
came back to me,
but as big as a house
as in Hieronymus Bosch.

Irresistibly it crushed
me out of the picture.
Who deserves more
for thirsting for blood?

This is that sparrow that
fell so hard for me, fell at my feet
while I slowly lowered the barrel
of my Red Ryder air rifle.

Forgive me, I'd think to say,
if continuing in that vein
wouldn't invite so many.
I wrapped him up tight

In a newspaper's cerements,
said, keep quiet about this.
But in the guilty aftermath,
returned to unbind

his heart from his bloodspot.
He flew. Life since is penitence.
Why kill a person?
A sparrow alone may be

the end of everything
for all who believe or don't
they're safe from the smother
of an expanding breast.

Walls

Look at that man bleeding
anything but ichor after trying
hard to be a god and stride ahead.
He forgot he might as well have stood
inside an empty drinking glass.

Only a world of no account
refuses to put up obstacles,
says the body is transitive,
smooths a path for the big brain.

A bus shelter's glass side wall,
to be plain, can't be hurried.
So look at the bumptious human,
wounded when things get real,
with a drop on the end of his nose
dependent as he is, such a baby.

Stop me. I'm talking to myself again,
and it's more like talking to a wall.
But in front of it and in back,
looking out and looking in,
I stand on both sides of this issue,
and being in two places at once
should be the prerogative of the god.
Look at me experiencing nature
while waiting for the miracle melt.

The Only

Struggling out of the stroller,
using his elbows, the little primitive
cannot be quieted or consoled.
Something is lost or missing
from his required list.
What is it? Toy or weapon,
whatever he had and now
does not have. The mother,
speaking to the back of his head,
wheeling him toward his majority,
says they'll get another one.
But the first one is the dear one.
Can this day be replaced?
Can his mother's voice from above be?
There are no other ones,
yet he can't tell her the blunt truth
and so continues as before.
He'll be less eruptive after.
In the evenings sometimes, sitting alone,
he'll lower the book he's been reading
and surprise himself with longing
for what nothing's ever made up for,
not love, not France, not glass houses.
And try to remember what it was.

Star Pupils

Sky flexing is lightning.
Let me put it this way,
the sky has its back turned
and its coat splits
along the middle seam.
So (a long susurrus),
the sky, looking away
from us, variously
starry-eyed or filmed
by clouds, or blank,
stares at vacancy.
Despite its blue composure
(the false front it puts on)
that keeps us humming,
a back adds little
to what we already know.
There are those who try for more,
brilliant pupils in green
forests on spiritual paths;
or, in provocative red socks,
going to the window
to see it's really true.

3

The Lion House

Every exhalation, every shifting muscle,
every paw-fall (the pad depressing)
raised the odor of the lion house.
It was the signature odor of the zoo.

And now to come on that odor again,
not in a park of pits and caves,
but thrown off by an encampment heaving
with men who've made a home away from home.

One day a man had to go there.
And now that he knows himself
no longer, he doesn't know it either.
You heard him shouting with the rest.

You went on after that.
You went on, and you had to ask
yourself what you'd gotten used to
like the lion house in your childhood.

Originals

Satan held the forest, but his lease was up.
To the gentlemanly ape and his English rose,
that put a different complexion on things.
Real property was the Word made flesh.

They laid claim to a land where no one was
who didn't run over the grass like foxes.
A folk so unclothed were nothing more than ghosts.
Moses set the precedent for mortmain.

Wasn't it yesterday they waded ashore in hip-boots?
The mothering gulls fussed: *You'll catch your death*.
But faith drains the bronchia of the justified man;
as the cannon backing him match his short fuse.

All in good time (a cottage homily),
the people of God make Boston, their servants
serve out Jacob's term, they knock down the fences
to branch out into the back country.

Why then do wolves sit on their tails and grin
at the settler's proper collar and rubber sword?
Why does the Indian, come again, weirdly
raise his arm in its wildcat's pelt?

But wordlessly the Indian turns on his heel.
The wolf does, too, sly boots, slipping away
into a night gnashing its stars at such as these.
All men are grass, these too shall pass, they say.

Winifred

Winifred our maid said
the movie house on Kennedy
Street is for white
people like you Larry.
I never heard that.

Winifred our maid said
she'd take me to see
whatever is on at the matinee
if I finished my American cheese sandwich.
I heard that.

Cat

No night passes without
a cry for help. A cat,
or what? Must be a cat,
it's in such a state. Some
concatenation of events
drove it to such a pitch.

You don't need to hear
its voice more than once;
the tone is plain. But better
start looking at things differently
if you want to know for sure
where this pain first broke from.

That was on its glide path, the building's
original lines like the frame of a stanza.
Warily it slipped into the interstices
of the construction like a white dotted
rhythm on a blueprint. You think
I'm making this up, but I tell you

a poor soul has ended here
still suffering a past indignity.
Hard to say what that was,
or why bearing up under it
was so impossible. A soul lost
long ago, lost or thrown away.

The Climate of Fascism

The dog that will bite,
ranging the stony yard,
chimes in when the wind
joins the chain-link fence.
On the high hill,
the wind is the air
in crisis, making the light
a real headache; the positive
immune to aspirin or reason.
In the house, tossed negligently
on a desk, coins of the realm
display the strongman's profile.
Can't we turn this around?
Grandmother, the last reader,
turning the page back to her girlhood.
Blurred blue flowers dot
the inside lip of her teacup.
But this day or that a waste-
pipe runs through the preserved
forest into the swimmers' lake.
And hidden in tough hedges
vipers like tire strips
slip out from the grinding heel
and strike. But don't say
you weren't warned by the one
pickled in a pharmacy window,
or afloat in sleep there, waiting.

Metatron's Journal

They've bombed the market for secondhand clothes.
The buyers, who were stained, now are spotless.
With what delicacy they'd selected
a lefthand suitcoat, an absent-minded shirt,
the very outfits that needed them the most.
The original owners, or their faintest breath and sweat,
lived on in what the poor now wore (but the holy have holes).
Clothed in virtue, they gave themselves a good shake
and sat down to drink tea out of crystal acorns.
At times, they glanced up at the sky as if the Twelfth
Imam might step down and rub the material
between two fingers to test a threadbare faith.
And yes, the figures on the wall had more geometry.
But drape the rattan chair, cover the bedroom mirror.

The Traveler

Finding a crease in the wall
joining two buildings, he turns
his back to the world to piss
in the middle of Wednesday.
That's no picnic for the Traveler,
or for anyone who has no place
to go to in his singularity.
But you've been around, you know how it is
when there's no one, so this is for you.
In kindergarten, bad actors
had to sit on their hands.
Use that as a memory;
it doesn't matter if it's not yours.
It can ease the tension you feel,
it's so tender; and it can move you
to a place inside your head (a phrase
no longer in vogue, but still
providing shelter when it rains). And listen:
Once I saw a nice German family
playing hide and seek
in the Berlin Holocaust Memorial's forest of stones.
Those people had a house and possessions.
Shake off the moment; distance is yours
I'm afraid, but you've darkened the earth.

What Is in the Water

I read the language they use, those words dropped
without a splash into the water of life
that we have to drink, that we drink to live,
predator, reaper, hellfire, the metal words.
And we make tea with them, we add them to soup;
we shower and soap and wash the children in them,
these remote lakes of fire for the others;
and we hose down the family car with them
and water the front lawn and our green plants
with them, with these invisible additives.
And if we do need to stomach them,
we couldn't imagine them to save our lives,
while our *aqua vita* envelops others in flames
and we continue using cups, dippers, glasses.

Tears

I think I'll move on into tears now,
not, like a Zeppelin, bursting into tears,
but moving the way stalled traffic loosens up
once the bodies are removed from the road.

They won't come from my eyes, these tears;
but every pore of my body will contribute their mite.
Why is for later. Meanwhile, you'll hardly catch
these tears in the act, as if you could detect

dew forming on a grassy lawn.
Dew reflects what it burns off into.
These tears I'm speaking of are opaque;
you can't look to them for anything.

And you wouldn't want to, since they spring
from such crazy places as my forehead
and the palms of my hands, quite unheard of,
totally lacking in grace or distinction.

Don't look at me, I'll be looking away,
blinded by the tears that run like sweat
or dew while that mortification lasts.
Sweat or dew or tears, who knows which?

Poor Fish

I saw the loser in 3-card Monte
pleading with the cat who ran the game:
You'll give me my fifty back, won't you?
Yesterday payday, rent today.
It's only fair, chance is unjust,
and this can't be happening to me,
can it? But above the avenue's rich rug
the cards continued changing places,
continued slicking through the dealer's practiced hands,
his dry eye out only for the police.

No one looking on or moving along
took the victim's part. Where in our
lapsed world do marks find pity?
Pity goes to animals, who can't help it,
and who try hard to stay away from us
unless a bright prospect entices them,
a lure for innocents. Like the pickerel
I caught who looked at me. Mutely
it beseeched me in the name of all that's holy
to save it. I ate it, soul and body.
But the hooked man, poor fish, voiced
his complaint and plea, for all the good that did him,
as I heard his cries grow fainter as I swam into
the shadows of towers dangling their lighted suites.

Fathers

God shook his head over a father
so suspiciously willing to kill the son
and end a line designed to break out
like seedlings from the pod.

So what if a voice ripped the night in two like paper?
It might have been the wind, not him.
Out of contempt he sent his servant
to wave the heavy cleaver away.

We prefer the father, he said,
who lets himself be pushed around by his grandchildren
as they splash on him in an inflatable wading pool
despite the blade, their age, hanging over his head.

At Sheepshead Bay

The chain-link fence cuts up the waters
it delimits; they're bite-size,
though who would dream of breaking
their teeth on wires? Certainly not my friend
tensed in a gray wooden deckchair

here, on his brief outing-with-nurse,
never more than steps from a door.
He bows his head listening for a signal
from his absence and receives it:
numbers he recites in confidence.

I see a figure drawn on a blackboard;
its original lines mist
and thrust ahead like chalk dust
under a pounding fist. I cough.
He says, "Two comes before three."

What links remain? Between what?
Hooking all ten fingers in them,
he might climb to the top of the fence,
as I did once at fifteen. I cut my palm.
I can't remember if I got over.

Walking

The child is as crisp and fresh
as a new pair of pants
whose two back pockets
are still buttoned,
but walking he feels his age.

Struggling to be human,
he staggers, to be precise.
Mother's hand slips out
of her warm ocelot muff,
but she stops herself from helping.

Father's double-breasted
belted overcoat tells
his son to be a man.
The sleepwalker lurches forward,
looking for the darkness he lost.

There's too much enlightenment
here, in the zoo they've taken him to;
it's full of claws and mouths.
Will the sidewalk lap him up
like the crocodile's white tongue?

He's rocky in his blue snowsuit;
he looks like one you point to
in a family photograph,
and say here, no later,
is where his troubles began.

In the Kingdom of the Chelonians

Turtle has her ear to the ground
and curls her lip. She knows
what's coming before we
appear, and that it's not justice but force
that tramps the earth and tramples
the small washed-up creatures
in the grass, in the forest,
in their houses getting dinner going.

Because turtle balances the world
on a thin shell, out of jealousy
others slaver over her liver that stores
a knowledge of gods and stars.
Pressed by such fierce circumstance
to a single begrudged heartbeat a minute,
to the least breath on the water's mirror,
she'll hide in mud as in a crowd.

What egotist could make her a lyre
or wring her out in a soup
or harness her like a mule
or have her race Achilles?
You'd never think of doing that
seeing her blossom out of the water,
beak and claws and Daoist eyes
sly with forbearance.

Turtles! They're not immortal,
yet they often outlive us.
Should we be hard-shelled or rueful
about going before they do?
When our feet stick in muck
they just go by the turtle book.
I see the turtle, and now I don't,
as she flips into the cold lake plop.

4

Advent

The white moth
down on its luck
in the hotel corridor

is a petty concern
or doesn't even
get under the wire

for anybody, booted,
crossing the threshold
of the breakfast room.

Wings outspread
as if in welcome,
the moth holds its breath.

But it's got thorax
written all over it.
So is anatomy fate?

A back window
giving on the garden
gave it a choice.

And don't think the moth
is a soul hankering
to rejoin the living.

The moth has a body
and is still all aflutter
in life, just like you,

o child of fortune.

Pebbles

These pebbles you step on or kick
in the mobbed Jewish cemetery,
what are they? Rejected prayers that rose
a little way at least and then fell back,
cooled to hardness by disappointment?
But they could never have got to that point.
They're too rough for such use,
and unintelligible, like letters in a word
no one's sentence could make sense of.
They dropped like teeth out of a mouth
that had opened to speak and was closed.
They strew the ground in front of stones
that winced under the names cut in them
like eyes now blind as steam irons.
The stones stand, persons among broken words;
those hard letters that need licking into shape.
Take up a single pebble from this alphabet
and put it back on the stone in your mouth.

This from That

Chalk dust puffs from the felt eraser
when I rub out an equation so offensive
it'll even take this number from that one
and we'll never see the first one again.
Like Bernard. I looked at his back in class,
but he'd dozed off behind the dashboard
last week before the driver hit the car ahead dead-on.
He lost face to the pixels of expressive glass.
Death by subtraction? He lived
but won't come back to class again.
Robert, too. A hard softball
knocked his breath out at recess
as if he were a rug on a clothesline.
Will my seat become vacant as well, I, chosen
to show the class pictures
of grass and trees, the things
that will always be there?
Such a dumb blond boy,
so mild in short sleeves,
smiling away his terror
about what happens if you take
one from one and he's the one.

A Parting

Camus casually waved goodbye
to his friend about to cross
a bridge in Paris. They assumed
Germans or no Germans,
they'd meet again soon. Neither did I
or my brother think the bad connection
on our phone call was such a span.
I said, "I'm losing you." And it's true,
our voices were more like waving than speaking.

The Annihilating Bicycle

Ten-speed, shiny, trim,
feminine, but no light or bell,
so sly, an annihilating beauty, a bright
shadow slicing under my shirt
to pass between ribs and the thin skin
covering them on the heart side
as if I were its all in all.

How intimate dying is.
Yet I put it off for now and put
an extra spoke in its wheel.
This jars the geared-up
Angel of Shivs, hairless
head shrunk down beneath
the handlebars as he wobbles by.

And I, feeling fine, I enter
a street where couples have long
kept in step and those all alone
walk thinking. They breathe
as if living, and I do, all of us
all eyes, all keeping an ear cocked
for the hiss at the heel of a racing tire.

My Last Deathbed

On my last deathbed I'll complain
I haven't gotten to the end
of the book I'd always had my nose in,
my life story. It would be wrong
to tell me how it ends before I get there.

But, as Rilke said, who will hear me?
Who else but a clanking military angel
pressed into service to perform this office?
He frowns down unsympathetically
at me in my crib with the sides up.

I tell him I want to put more mileage
on the car without more wear and tear.
(A car's universal appeal is my symbol.)
Give me the last word and the say when
to utter it and to whom. It won't be you.

I'll add that last for good measure,
however sternly deaf like all boilerplate angels
this towhead Swede draftee proves to be.
But what *is* my last word? What should I say?
I have to think. I need time to think.

Ants

The good times are over,
said the ant to itself.
It couldn't see as far
as the crushed grass ahead,
but it felt the impact
of a fine-grade shadow
there was no way out of.
And so it proved: the ant
gave up its territory.
The ant's name has been lost,
and no one claimed the body
for burial and memorial.
The stamping man, however,
went on to better things
before he too fell underfoot.
The moral is true but banal,
and true because it is banal.
But the reader shuts his book.
He finds it a place on the shelf
where he won't have to see it again.
Am I supposed to be an ant? He asks.
The Sisters of Dew hear him
all the way outside on the lawn,
but quietism is their métier.
Rather than comment, they send
their condolences, inaudibly,
and he puts on his pajamas.

The Milkweed Diet

In the sixth chapter
God sets the Monarch
butterfly the task
of cracking a person's
lifeline with its two wings
when it's time.

In his prayer book
the old man reads
the Blessing for Milkweed,
every sterling thread of which
is essential to the Monarch's diet,
and his faith is tested.

He'd starve the insect
to go on living
endless hours, endless days.
Didn't the widows say he looked sixty?
In his book,
birds snap butterflies out of the air.

But one flutter
makes a stir and changes everything—
slightly, yet a little is enough
for God to turn his face from him.
The butterflies have started eating,
they're eating, it's over.

Bearing Grandma

What a fantastic undertaking,
carrying out the old lady,
who alternately felt light
as a bouquet of spring flowers
and heavy as a fire iron.
How strange to remove her from her upstairs bedroom
and bundle her along the landing,
together the men raising her at an angle
above the oak banister;
then turning their wrists
(the first man moving onto the highest step),
to point the corpse down the staircase
feet first, so that the blood
wouldn't rush to her head.
But on reaching the sunlit foyer,
they paused; as if she'd asked them to
so that she could get a last look
at the picture on the wall,
and a pair of bronzed baby shoes
one of her absent children had worn.
But the interruption was brief;
in her life she'd never been maudlin.
Besides, the limousine she'd ordered
had just found the right address.

Elegy

The Bardo's lights are signs
running the length of the strip mall
unfolding like a paper dragon
after Four Corners on a dark
day along the road of excess.
Farther back is the tower apartment
whose occupant lost ground fast.
He moves on, but we go back
by means of some lucky metaphysic
as green as skinning the cat
and find his absence behind his door.
It's in his pillow's hollow and his clear
syllables still ready to be switched on.
But also in black mold in the bathtub
the endlessly replenishing source
of a starless and dreamless night.
There no one's eyes light up
to see before him the face he loved,
and the tongue is like wet feathers.
The person who came to this pretty pass
has wandered off and stopped responding.
Remember him. Because if you don't, who will?
Short, square, functional, is all.
Bending near the end to touch the earth
as if a spark might ignite
his index finger to raise his temperature.
We knew better, but who are we?
Some people used to believe the dead
needed our help to give them some spine.
They flounder around like blind dolls,
jumbled together, wearing the wrong clothes
or none at all. For a short while
we make much of him.
Then that time is past.

The History of Earthworms

I was ashamed of living
before I'd lived a little.
My eyes bent to the ground
as I slid on grass or padded
in forbidden mud, there
where earthworms were.

They were unsubtle to come up
after rain, spluttering mutely,
drowning in puddles thinner
than a thumbnail.
I helped them out and relished
their crawling at my feet.

Fearing they'd snap like glass
straws before I did them the favor,
I pushed and pulled but gently.
Their properties were a study
for one so ignorant of ends
when it came to bodies.

Gradually I'd grow closer
to what else squirmed.
But worms were unsocial
and didn't bite or carp.
Persecuted the same,
weren't we blood brothers?

We were worms, not serpents,
though both shyly retreat.
I grew up mild as milk
as one of them. Then not.
I stood on my own two feet,
not watching where my foot fell.

At the end, I can't get worse
as I fall off my high horse.
I expect to see eye to eye
with earthworms again, see
the luster I saw back then when
what was beneath me wasn't.

Mercury

The way Bach's last fugue stops
is the way you want to,
with everything going just fine up to then.

The fox picked off the kittens, one by one.
The mother cat, missing them, mewed,
searched, came up empty, forgot them.

Inadequately strained leaves of the tea plant
float in the cup to remind me
that nothing should go down too easily.

The cashier tells me she puts sugar cookies
in her microwave, but I can't believe
this is a sexual invitation.

She killed the porcupine eating her car tires
with the spade she later used to bury it.
Her moral position was complex.

Her red hair was so red
it had obviously been
indoctrinated with the need to be red.

She's gone, and look at the way my sock is rumpled.
Did it ever have any elastic
to lose? It did if I did.

"You can't fight your whole life,"
Stanley says to the concessionaire,
who tells him that is wisdom.

We owe everything to the past.
My aunt bought my mother
a nightgown for her honeymoon.

Death will disappoint you like your wife.
She calls long distance; you answer joyfully;
she says turn the radio down.

The fern branch cut into the handle
of the saw purely as decoration
helps me to get a grip.

Wheeling over the transfer station,
exercising their right to criticize,
the crows say what a dump it is.

The horse lifts one foot, fastidiously,
from the current flowing under him,
and over him, and through him.

Lying awake in the dark this morning,
I think of a star that's far away and pulling
even farther away from me.

The noise I make running back upstairs
for an umbrella gives the walls
time before I burst in to pull themselves together.

A man carrying a danger sign
is someone to look out for
and be careful of.

We didn't believe he would kill himself
because he had never done anything like that before,
although there's a first time for everything.

Fashion models and recent corpses
stare at each other in disbelief
from the newspaper's facing pages.

Like an artist who's ahead of his time,
the beggar hisses in exasperation
when his work goes unappreciated.

The tide withdraws; the naked ground
anxiously talks about its illness,
whether it will come back.

The bee that stung me came off the back of a plate
in the Berlin Porcelain Museum
to say nature beats culture.

Nobody can see me
until I put on
my glasses.

Thursday is a thirsty day,
says the child, who doesn't know
to leave well enough alone.

The intellectual's severed head advises
the executioner to read his books. He does, but the pages
he licks his fingertip to turn are poisoned.

The armored car driver had to slam his door
twice before it stayed shut
Such things give me pause.

The wind raised by passing cars
is full of every imaginable filth
and stirs the day lilies.

A woman lying
with her legs raised
invites comparison.

That girl in her sundress
will grow out of the interrogative mode
and become the bearded lady.

Are you the sparrow found in Gozzoli,
found, as usual, in a lower corner,
looking for a crumb off-canvas?

This woman is her own project;
she indents the air, which then
talks in paragraphs to praise her.

The gold sprinkles on the Greek vases
need the discarded cigar's gold band
to complete the history of mannerism.

Listening to the silver paper crinkle
while laughing over sugar candy
made the day more than bearable.

Drinking grape soda from a bottle
held up against a purple sunset is decadent,
as those things go.

Thieves break into a neon factory
and steal mercury to dip their cigarettes in
so that the god will be immanent.

To wake with the pillows on the floor
and leaves inside the bedroom door,
and your foot, like a statue's, clearly broken.

I'm just thinking of the sky,
the faces it makes, it's silence
that is tired of my voice.

Nurses unnerve me,
smoking Kools
on the hospital steps.

When the doctor approaches the bedside,
the nurses fall back and huddle together,
gossiping like village wives.

He pointed to his burial ground
as we drove by in the rain. Turning too late,
I read the sign NORMAN'S FARM MART.

You could pick up that bare tree
in your hand, it seems so close
and so small, and comb your hair with it.

I watched a woman kissing a man in the street.
When their faces parted, she smiled all over hers.
She had had to stand on tiptoe to reach his lips.

I like what happens to the muscles in your face,
and to your eyes as well,
as you walk along the street eating an apple.

I want to be forgiven at 4 a.m.,
forgiven like the green plant on the table
when its still too dark to see it for what it is.

Low murmurs. Muted piano.
The screened porch. A summer evening.
Who would want to complete these sentences?

It must have been past three.
A bird in the uncut grass removed its shadow.
The true self emerged.

The rain is trying to get to the sea,
but it keeps being thrown back
on rivers and streams and swampy grasslands.

The cicadas call out numbers
to the crickets, who chant
the alphabet back at them.

The scarlet tanager in the plum tree
is too much to take,
though a bare minimum when the snows arrive.

The flies on the windowsill were poised
as only the dead can be. Somewhere out in the field,
as seen from the window . . .

Like it or not, your identity sticks to you
like a moth to the door screen,
where it attached itself the night before.

Never allow yourself to be photographed
smiling triumphantly. That picture
will illustrate your obituary.

It was so hot the birds' colors ran.
More, the willows were demoralized.
Worst of all, the clouds folded.

The goldfinch shot across the garden party
like the glass of champagne a woman
jealously threw at her fleeing spouse.

Consider the man whose chute didn't open
yet who lived by giving in to his end so completely
that the earth refused to punish gentleness.

If it happened to you, it happened only to you.
If it happened to others, it didn't happen to you.
If it didn't happen to you, it didn't happen.

One Last Thing

When my words are lost, twisted
by wind-devils, are puffed away
like ash or dust, those words
I wanted to leave an impression
on the air with, and that didn't
make a dent, when the room

pressing my images to make something
of themselves is wreckage or worse,
the house down, the city abandoned
by those who've gone to the country
and are never coming back, then,
if someone somewhere is still alive

to the concentration of emotion
in language, they may remember me,
not me but my outline, not that
but the balanced distress of one
who rose to the height of his downfall
and was visible in words to himself.

About the Author

Lewis Meyers (1934–2020) lived a capacious life dedicated to art, music, teaching, and politics—but his true love was poetry. As a graduate student studying with Donald Hall, he published in such august journals as *Paris Review*, *Poetry Northwest*, and *Hudson Review*. But after these early successes, he gave little energy to seeking recognition. During his years teaching in the English Department at Hunter College (1970–2008), he continued writing poems but seldom submitted them. Several did appear, however—*Antioch Review*, *Field*, and *Literary Review*. After he retired from teaching in 2008, he dedicated himself exclusively to writing poems. Echoing Joan Mitchell's characterization of the place of painting in her life, he called writing poems an "addiction." Since his death, his poems have appeared in the *Paris Review*, *Hudson Review*, *Five Points*, *Massachusetts Review*, *Poetry Northwest*, *Plume*, and *Arkansas International*.

Photograph of the author by
Diana Tietjens Meyers.
Used by permission.

Free Verse Editions

Edited by Jon Thompson

Ghost Letters by Baba Badji

Go On by Ethel Rackin

Here City by Rick Snyder

I Am Not Korean by Song Kyeong-dong

An Image Not a Book by Kylan Rice

Instances: Selected Poems by Jeongrye Choi, trans. by Brenda Hillman, Wayne de Fremery, & Jeongrye Choi

Interglacial by Tracy Zeman

Invitatory by Molly Spencer

Last Morning by Simon Smith

The Magnetic Brackets by Jesús Losada, trans. by M. Smith & L. Ingelmo

Man Praying by Donald Platt

A Map of Faring by Peter Riley

The Miraculous Courageous by Josh Booton

Mirrorforms by Peter Kline

M O 月 N by Chengru He

A Myth of Ariadne by Martha Ronk

No Shape Bends the River So Long by Monica Berlin & Beth Marzoni

North | Rock | Edge by Susan Tichy

Not into the Blossoms and Not into the Air by Elizabeth Jacobson

Overyellow, by Nicolas Pesquès, translated by Cole Swensen

Parallel Resting Places by Laura Wetherington

pH of Au by Vanessa Couto Johnson

Physis by Nicolas Pesquès, translated by Cole Swensen

Pilgrimage Suites by Derek Gromadzki

Pilgrimly by Siobhán Scarry

Poems from above the Hill & Selected Work by Ashur Etwebi, trans. by Brenda Hillman & Diallah Haidar

The Prison Poems by Miguel Hernández, trans. by Michael Smith

Puppet Wardrobe by Daniel Tiffany

Quarry by Carolyn Guinzio

remanence by Boyer Rickel

Republic of Song by Kelvin Corcoran

Rivermouth Shouting by Jean Gallagher

Rumor by Elizabeth Robinson

Saint with a Peacock Voice by L. S. Klatt

Settlers by F. Daniel Rzicznek

A Short History of Anger by Joy Manesiotis

Signs Following by Ger Killeen

Small Sillion by Joshua McKinney

Split the Crow by Sarah Sousa

www.ingramcontent.com/pod-product-compliance
Lightning Source LLC
Chambersburg PA
CBHW031144090426
42738CB00008B/1217